How to Self- Manage Rental Property

for
Maximum Profit$
&
Minimum Stress

Francis R. Calleon

Realtor, BBA, SRES, GRI

The Real Estate Pub, LLC

Printed in the United States of America

ISBN-10: 0692574891

ISBN-13: 978-0692574898

10 9 8 7 6 5 4 3 2

Empire Publishing

www.empire-publishing.com

Table of Contents

Introduction

Welcome to my book on "How to Self-Manage Rental Property for Maximum Profits and Minimum Stress."

If you already own property and manage it well, this will be a great refresher, and if not, this will be an eye-opener on things that went wrong in the past and how it could have been prevented. This book will connect you to my website and database so you can stay abreast on laws, trends, markets, new technologies, etc.

Most authors on this subject will tell you similar things, but everyone has unique experiences. This is what I give to you - My experience over the past 30 years of managing real estate properties, mostly my own.

About the Author

As the author, I have over 23 years of full-time Real Estate experience in Property Management, Residential Sales, Commercial Sales and Commercial Leases.

I currently teach clients and potential clients how to identify, purchase and manage their investment property from beginning to end, and all the in-betweens, to ensure a steady source of passive income. Passive income is defined as unearned income, whereby, you don't have to be present to earn it.

I also assist clients in managing their real estate portfolio, which includes purchasing, managing, exchanging (1031) and planning for long-term passive income during retirement.

Preface

This book was designed for those of you who already have an investment property that you have had for a while, have recently inherited, have recently purchased or will soon have.

The intent of this book is to make the highest and best use of the property you have and turn it into a profit-generating asset.

If you are planning on purchasing an investment property in the future to become a landlord and gain passive income, you can soon purchase my next book "How to Buy an Investment Property for a Great Cash Flow!" at http://www.realestateplushawaii.com.

This book "How to Self-Manage Rental Property for Maximum Profits and Minimum Stress," is designed to develop your skills to a practical level in the areas of designing, marketing, interviewing, negotiating, maintaining and managing.

By the way, even if you plan to use a Property Manager because you don't have the time to manage it yourself, you should read this book anyway. It will help you in selecting a competent Property Manager.

Enjoy the resource!

How to Self- Manage Rental Property for Maximum Profits & Minimum Stress

Chapter One

Getting Your Place Ready to Show

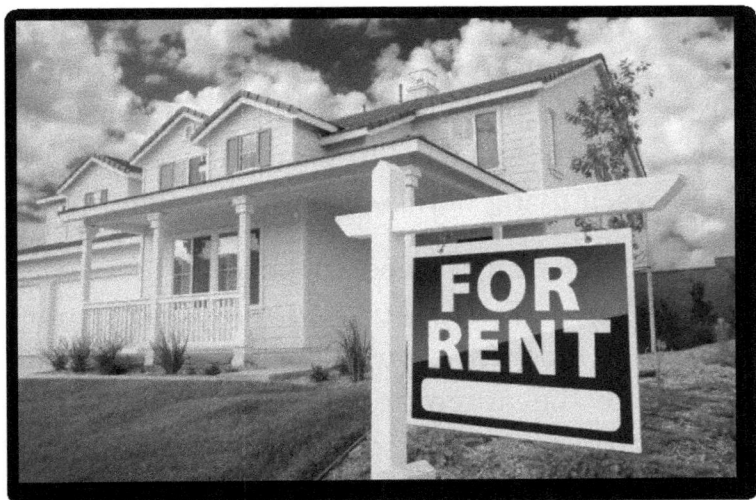

If there is anything that you should remember from this chapter, it's this...

"WOW" Factor!

Keep reading to find out what I mean by this.

Now that you have made the decision to become a landlord and manage your own property, you want to attract tenants. To do this you MUST create the "WOW" factor that radiates from your property, and this means that you need to prepare it properly by fixing, cleaning, upgrading and staging. In reality, you want to create a model living environment so when the potential tenant previews the property – the first word out of their mouth is "WOW!" Translation? "I can see myself living here! – Where do I sign?"

Two (2) things need to happen to create this "WOW." First, you need to upgrade your unit with modern, cleaner & simpler looks. It needs to be uncluttered and look like a model. ("Easy for you to say, you say?") Yes, I know you have a budget but, if you keep this concept in mind and work with your budget, you'll be surprised at how great you can make the place look. Use some elbow grease as well! Low-cost items include paint, caulking, cleaners, etc.

If your budget calls for it, you should update/upgrade items that need it. An example of this would be to install new wood laminate flooring to replace old and worn carpet, or new kitchen countertops to replace old and stained Formica. In addition, your local hardware store may offer inexpensive window coverings.

The second thing is to stage your property as your budget will allow. It can be as simple as a potted plant, a chair & table in the corner, with a flower vase on the counter, or you can do a fully furnished interior with a bedroom set, living room set, dining table & chairs, etc. or somewhere in-between.

Here are a few tips to help attract these potential tenant(s) to your property by incorporating some "WOW" factor concepts:

•Think of the type of property you have: If you have a luxury property, you are looking to attract high-end tenants that are really not ready to purchase a place. They intend to stay temporary until they get a re-assignment or until they become familiar enough with the town to know where they want to live. So, there is definitely a market for these high-end tenants and they want a high-end property look. This is where staging comes in, go to www.houzz.com to see techniques on staging for the high-end and get some ideas.

In all likelihood, if you have a high-end property, you can probably afford to hire a professional to upgrade, rent and manage your property. Well, you can still upgrade with lower cost and creative methods. For some ideas, go to:

http://www.thisoldhouse.com

•Think of the location of your property: Close to the Business District, near a University, in Suburbia or in the country. Think of who your potential tenants are (e.g. If they are students, then stage the unit with furniture conducive to their life- style: utility/dining table, larger coffee table, a desk in the corner, reading lamps, large microwave oven, and durable flooring. For home staging tips, go to:

www.HGTVDecorating.com

or

www.RealtorMag.realtor.org/home-and-design/staging-tips

•Stage the place with simplicity & purpose; you want a place you would want to call home. You want the furniture to fit adequately the size of your place and match the décor. You can go to a website to select furniture suitable for your unit, such as:

http://www.rentwow.com

Many of these furniture rental companies give you the option to purchase the furniture. Of course, some kind of equitable negotiations need to take place between you and your tenant, such as a higher rent, a long-term lease, paying the utilities, etc.

•Pastel colors and patterns on the walls are used to accentuate the already "awesome" features. By adding color to the walls and trim, the limited space will appear brighter and larger. It could also create a particular mood appropriate for each room. For example, in one of my condos, I painted the dining area off of the kitchen, a salmon shade. In my opinion, this gave it a warmer, softer glow to the room and enhanced the appetite. Well, it helped to sell the unit anyway.

•It really helps if you stimulate all the senses, such as the sense of smell with pleasant & inviting aromas; baked bread, lavender scents, cinnamon, apple pie, etc. For the eyes – bouquet of roses, green & live plant arrangements, colors, etc.

•Mirrored closet doors and a closet organizer are ALWAYS a PLUS. Not only does the room appear larger and brighter, but it also appears more organized and upscale. People can see them storing their things here and there if you sway them to think that way.

•When staging the property, remember, less is more efficient, that is. You want to furnish & accessorize the property to a point in which the prospective tenant can see how the property can be furnished.

The more simplistic the furniture, the more of a positive impact it will make, especially if the place is on the smaller side. There are space-friendly furnishings available.

For great ideas that you could find in your local furniture market, go to:

www.wimp.com/spacesaving/

Also, for ideas on Murphy beds and the like, go to:

www.hiddenbed.com

An option is to rent your place fully-furnished for the tenants who have little or no furniture. In some instances, the renters, in order to save on shipping costs, will sell their furniture rather than ship it to their new location. This will save you the time and hassle of removing your furniture after the lease is signed. Of course, this greater investment of furnishings could be reflected in higher rents. Another upside to this is that you won't have to remove the furniture and find a place to store it.

If you do need to remove all the furniture, you should have a plan on where to store it for later use. You can also use them in another investment property or use it in your own residence. I have a spare room where I keep staged furniture, and I don't miss it when it's gone.

Now, if your real estate market is not a transient one, and you know you will be housing more of the local population, usually with their own furniture, there are staging companies that will do the temporary staging for you, but for a price. These companies usually offer the option of buying the furniture. They will even include artwork. Every county has professional stagers online for estimates let your fingers do the walking and get their costs and available services. To learn more about staging, go to:

http://www.lushome.com/modern-furniture-small-spaces-15-great-ideas decorating-small-apartments-homes/107141

REMEMBER: The prospective tenant needs to immediately visualize living in this property and seeing how well they will fit in. Now, if they just invested in a brand new living room set or bedroom set and it's just too big for your property, there's probably nothing you can do to secure a lease with them as your new tenant.

Chapter Two

Advertising and Marketing

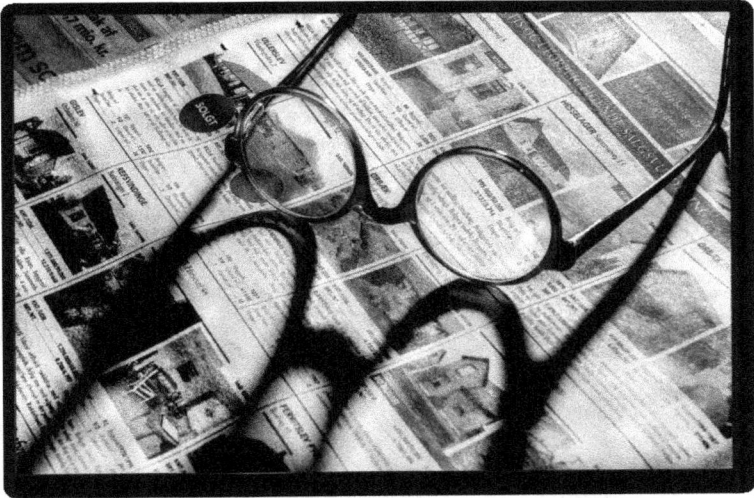

Now that you have your property staged to attract the right perspective tenant, it is time to advertise and market your property to find that right tenant and gain passive income!

The following are a few tips on where to advertise.

•Think of the publications & media forums that will best attract the type of tenant you desire. If you are advertising a property in the outskirts of town, stick to local publications in the area: Craig's List, Zillow, Trulia and the local newspaper. It's also inexpensive, if not free, to do this. Don't advertise this listing in the Luxury Magazine, Home & Land or business publications since the readership is low for your prospective tenant. It is very expensive to run ads there and these are monthly publications, which have specific deadlines to submit your investment property ad & may be featured in a later, instead of current, issue.

•Craigslist is always a popular venue and results are almost always guaranteed. However, you must remember to renew your posting daily or at least every two days to avoid your ad getting buried amongst the numerous postings uploaded daily. Currently, you can load up to 24 pictures and create the write-up as lengthy as you like. The website is www.craigslist.com, and you will need to select your state. For tips on writing a good ad, go to my website:

http://www.realestateplushawaii.com.

•Your local newspaper is another way to advertise your rental property. The benefits of this venue would be that it is accessible to the prospective tenant in both print (hardcopy) and digital via the internet. Go to, for example, www.staradvertiser.com or your local newspaper. Even though we live in the 21st century and are considered the age of technology, there are many people who either do not have access to a computer or still prefer the hardcopy version. You'd be surprised at the number of non-techies out there, especially the older generation, pre-baby boomers that may never have adapted to the change.

•Another avenue to advertise is in various real estate publications that are usually housed on the kiosks in the malls and markets. However, these publications are also monthly and are not as current as Craig's List or the daily paper that renews its ads consistently. By the time people get it and call, the listing is outdated. However, most of these publications have on-line access that the public can view.

The most important thing here is to price your rent properly according to the market demand. Start with the asking rents for similar places to your unit.

If you don't get any calls, or only a few, for the first week, you may consider reducing the rent by 3% - 5% until you do. Of course, your goal is to have a positive cash flow over your expenses, so proper pricing of the rent is imperative. Refer to my other book on "How to Buy an Investment Property for a Great Cash Flow!" to vastly improve your likelihood of a positive cash flow.

Chapter Three

Selecting the Tenant

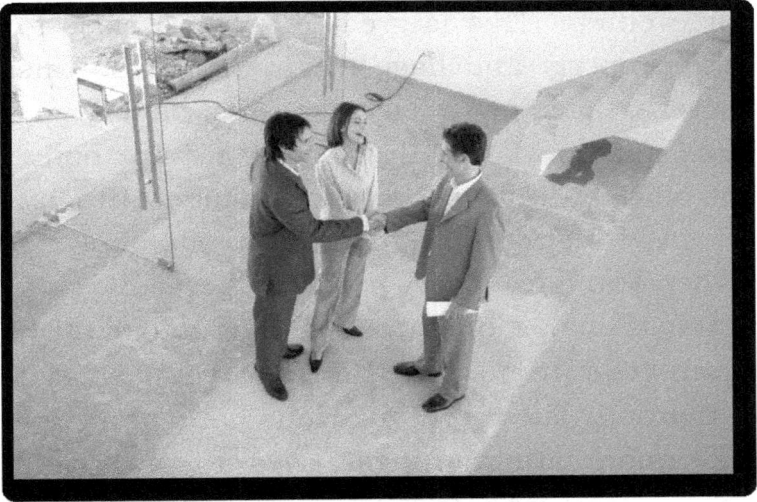

Alright, so far so good, you advertised, and the prospective tenants' were very interested – they're calling. I will discuss in this chapter how to show the property, how to screen the prospects, how to analyze your choices, how to interview and how to select the best tenant.

Here are a few ways that I recommend that you set up showings to get results.

Individual Showing– As each interested tenant calls, you show the property that day or evening. (This is great if you are close to the property and have the luxury to do this several times per week or even per day). Many investors work mostly at their nearby home or office as this would be convenient. In fact, I would highly recommend a private showing when you have a very good prospect, maybe a professional, a business manager, etc, so you can be sure to give him/her your special attention. The more luxurious your property, the more attention you need to give your prospective tenants.

Small Groups– When you receive a few interested tenants contacting you in one day, you may then want to set up a time for the small to medium group to meet you at the property. In this way, you will make sure everyone previews the place in one appointment and not be overwhelmed by too many prospects. This is okay especially when most in the group have the same socioeconomic background and you expect the property to rent quickly. You can always reschedule an individual appointment after your first group meeting if you meet a prospect that you really like and have a good rapport with. If your property is in an area that commands lower rents, you still need to be discerning about their ability to pay the rent regularly and keep the property in good condition. I'll discuss more on this in later in this chapter.

Mass Showing– This is when you have lots of interest or very high demand and inform all the perspective tenants that you will be showing the property on a specific date and between certain times. You can schedule a 2-4 hour window and assign people to a ½ hour time slot in order to balance the showings and give quality time for showing.

This could be the best way if you have such a busy schedule, more than one property to show and limited times that you can be at the property. Getting an assistant to help with the applications, log-ins and answer questions will be extremely helpful in this instance.

Now you have met all the prospective tenants and have the applications and credit reports, it is time to analyze the information and make your selection. Before I go any further with this section, I would like to include few tips that helped me with a quality tenant selection:

1. While the goal is to get the right tenant quickly, it is okay to not make a selection on the first go-round if you are not sure that you have your "ideal" tenant. This might be the difference between you and a property manager, who might be only interested in collecting rental fees as soon as possible and cutting advertising expense. Remember, this is your property, and you want to feel comfortable with your selection - someone that has the best likelihood of paying the rent every month on time, taking care of your property and conducting themselves in a civil manner. Yes, you need the income/cash flow, which is why you are doing this in the first place, but, trust me, it could be more

costly if you make a wrong selection. Check out www.mytenantfromhell.com to give you some idea of what I mean.

2. When you review the applications and their credit reports, rank the applicants and have selected your model tenant, then contact them as soon as possible. This is because your property is probably not the only one the applicant previewed. Also, if you find the right tenant and wait too long to contact the applicant to offer the place, chances are the applicant will have already secured a lease with another landlord. In reality, many landlords go by gut-feel when selecting prospective tenants and don't do their due-diligent checks, like, calling previous landlords, analyzing credit reports or calling their immediate supervisor to verify employment. Do your homework and do it quickly so you can offer them the unit before you lose them.

3. It is important to state your selection criteria at the start. To minimize the likelihood of legal disputes against you, remind the applicant that, as you mentioned

at the showing, your selection will be based on only two criterion: 1) Your perceived ability to consistently pay the rent based on income, tenure on the job, probability of continued employment, etc. (e.g. An Executive type or other Professional would likely tip the scale. 2) Past conduct as a tenant. In other words, if a previous landlord says that there were many complaints about excessive noise or illegal parking or disruptive behavior, you would likely turn him/her away as your new tenant. Remember that the previous landlord has more credibility that the current landlord, who may be trying to get rid of him/her.

4. Ask the prospective tenant to bring a copy of his or her credit report. They can get it at:

www.freecreditreport.com

www.freescoreonline.com

www.annualcreditreport.com

If you investigate these reports further, you want to get one that provides the derogatory for each person. These are the

30/60/90 indicators that refer to the number of times late payments exceeded 30 days/60 days/90 days. This will give you an excellent picture of how reliable the individual is on paying anything on time.

5. There is Local and National Fair Housing Laws that we need to comply with. See the following websites. For the Hawaii Fair Housing Act, go to:

www.fairhousinghawaii.org

For the National Fair Housing Act, go to:

www.civilrights.org/fairhousing/laws/

Again, it's important to remind the tenant on your selection criteria, and their past negative behavior.

Now that you have selected the right tenant for your property, it is time to personally secure a lease.

I'm not saying that there is a crystal ball for knowing for sure that this is the "dream" tenant – things still can go bad in the future! We all know that there are people out there that are very skilled at hiding their inequities and past negative behavior. We do our best with credit report (with derogs), phone calls to landlords, personal interviews and verification of employment. Legally, that's really all you can do, but it gives us a good shot and making a quality selection.

Chapter Four

Securing the Lease

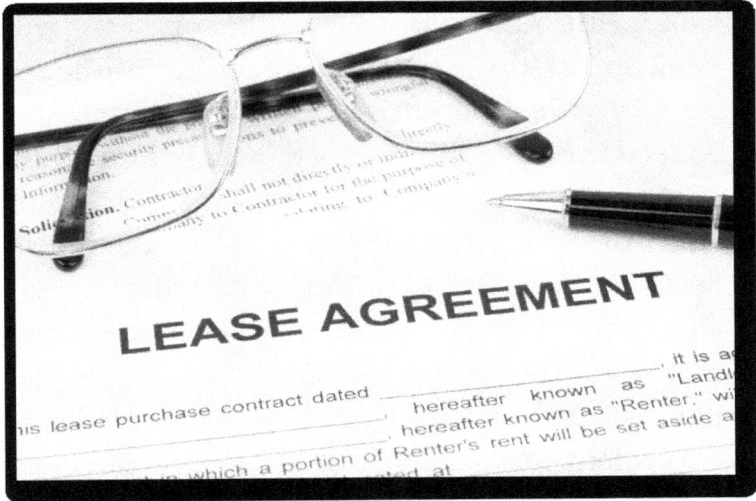

Now that you've staged your property, advertised & marketed your property, selected the "right" tenant for your property, you now need to secure that INCOME, by securing the lease.

Again, you want to meet the chosen tenant as quickly as possible, like, that afternoon or 1st thing in the morning. Remember, you don't want another landlord to have ample time to steal this great tenant away from you.

So, secure the lease and start getting your "passive income!" When you call to give the wonderful news to the applicant, you will need to set up a meeting to review the lease for all parties' signatures, initials & dates and collect the security deposit, which is usually one month's rent. Every state has a different rule or law that governs the maximum security deposit that you can collect. For example, Hawaii just recently allowed the equivalent of (2) month rent, if you permit a pet in the property. The extra month equivalent is designated as a Pet Security Deposit.

Your state may vary from this. Look it up on the state website that reads www.(state)govermnemt.gov.

In any case, make sure that you insist on a Cashier's Check for the security deposit and first-month's rent combined, for "security purposes."Nothing is worse than turning over the keys, fob, remotes, all docs, then discovering that their personal check bounced. WHAT NOW!

Now for the necessary paperwork. You will need to procure a Rental Docs Packet, which has six (6) rental docs that include:

1. Rental Agreement

2. Lead-Based Paint Addendum

3. Property Condition Form

4. Check-Out Form

5. Addendum of Basic House Rules (plus condo House Rules, if applicable)

6. Items-to-Tenant List

Go to www.therealestatepub.com to access these docs.

There are several areas to consider when preparing the lease agreement.

First – The Length of the Lease: At this point, it was more likely that the lease term was already verbally agreed upon, but here are slight ramifications to the duration of the lease terms.

1) A 1 to 5-month lease is only an option if you are considering becoming a vacation-type rental, which is considered, in a state like Hawaii, a short term lease. What this means is that your property will be like a hotel or bed & breakfast in which you will be subject to paying the TAT (Transient Accommodation Tax). Currently it is at 9.25%, with ongoing proposals to revise it. (Check with your state laws on short-term renters)

1. A 6-month lease will avoid the TAT because that is considered a long-term lease. This is usually an optimal time period, especially if the rental market is booming upward. It will provide you with an opportunity to increase the rent to the rising market rate after six months Remember to give 45-days written notice per the Landlord-Tenant Code. It also gives you enough time as a landlord to confirm if this is the tenant you want to keep, since it's not too long to "bite the bullet" should things not work out

(Chapter 6 will discuss tenant removal). Besides, at the end of the lease, if neither party gives notice to terminate the rental agreement, the terms automatically turn into a month-to- month agreement. Again, you do not want to be in a contractual agreement with a tenant for a year if after a few months you realize that it was a bad selection.

2. A 1-year lease is great during a rental market that is slow or if you are relatively certain, upfront, that this is the tenant you want to keep. Even if the rent was less than desirable, you will still be getting a steady monthly income for the year. If you have a great tenant at the end of the lease, both parties may be interested in renewing a longer lease term at a new fixed rent amount. This will give both sides peace of mind for another year.

Once you determined the terms, gather all applicable forms, agreements and documents prior to meeting the tenant, you need to sign. Here are "Must Have" documents to bring with you, with a copy for the tenant.

•Rental Agreement

- Landlord-Tenant Code Handbook

- Fair Housing Overview Packet

- Photos of the property for review and initials

- Addenda (Pet, Landlord Rules & Regulations, Individual Policies, Acknowledgements, etc.)

- Lead-Based Paint Addendum & Pamphlet (If your property has been built prior to 1979). This is Federal Law.

- Copy of the House Rules (If applicable, for condos, as well.)

- Items-to-Tenant List (Keys, FOBs, House Rules, Landlord-Tenant Code Handbook, Condo Docs, etc.) The tenant will need to sign a receipt for these items.

- Copy of the Subdivision Rules (If applicable) Usually, a single-family dwelling subdivision will have something called CC&R's (Covenants, Conditions & Restrictions) that governs the Do's, Don'ts, Cant's and conduct of the dwellers within that subdivision. The idea is to keep the value of the subdivision by putting in place rules to keep primarily the aesthetics high.

Chapter Five

Managing & Solving Problems

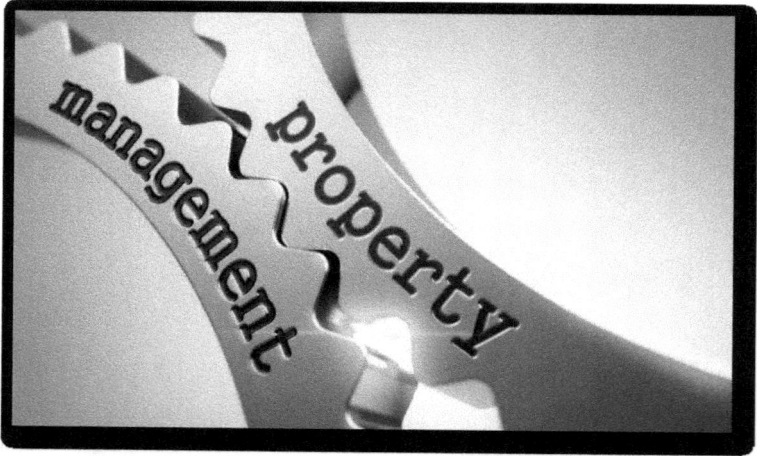

At last! You now have selected a great tenant, secured a sound lease, and you have the security deposit. You turned over the keys to the new tenant of your property and, collected the 1st month's rent. HOORAY, CASH FLOW!

This chapter is to provide tips for developing a great landlord-tenant relationship that will go a long way in managing both your tenant and your property. Everything from managing your cash flow to solving problems will be discussed.

If the tenant feels that you are a person who cares about their well-being, they will try to abide by your wishes and respect your property. They will also be reluctant to move to even a better place, if they perceive you as a good landlord.

Here are some extremely helpful hints on managing your property and solving problems:

•Always respond immediately to their concerns, whether you approve them or not. If you leave them "hanging," they may feel as if you don't care about them and, as a result, may not take care of your needs, which includes paying rent and taking great care of your property. If there's a problem, get it fixed right away. Feeling respected goes both ways.

•Remember them on Thanksgiving and Christmas, by sending them a small gift or an email greeting. Remembering their birthday won't hurt either.

•Make sure that YOU read and understand the Landlord-Tenant Code Handbook. Believe me, the tenant has, more than likely, studied and memorized this document.

Contained therein, are the rights and expectations of both the Landlord and the Tenant.

http://files.hawaii.gov/dcca/ocp/landlord_te nant/landlord-tenant-handbook.pdf

•Make sure you also read and understand the Lead-Based Paint Addendum and the Pamphlet (This applies if your property was built prior to 1979). This is a Federal disclosure requirement.

http://www2.epa.gov/lead/protect-your-family-lead-your-home-real-estate-disclosure

•Read and understand the Fair Housing Act

http://www.fairhousinghawaii.org/ (Hawaii)

http://www.civilrights.org/fairhousing/laws/
(National)

I know this was discussed during the Selection Process but stay abreast with updates and new concerns that can lead to new laws. The more awareness you have, the less likely you will cross the line, even if you have no intentions to do so.

•Read and understand the House Rules (for condos) or Subdivision Rules (for a House) and remember, the addenda that the tenant acknowledged, signed & dated is in addition to your House Rules. (Your separate addenda will mean that you have the right to be stricter with your property than the House or Subdivision Rules). A good example of this is, if the condo building allows pets, you still have a right not to allow them in your unit. I know it makes the rule a lot more difficult to govern, so you need periodic inspections to insure compliance.

If you recall Chapter 3 on tenant selection, if the tenant says, "I have pet, but I'm going to give it up or leave it with my sister.", you may want to check up on them or just not take the risk at all; I'm sure you can come up with a legitimate reason to select someone else.

•Conduct periodic inspections of your property so you can see if there are any repairs or issues that need to be addressed. Many tenants are not very good about reporting repair problems. This can easily be accomplished through a routine periodic inspection for termites, plumbing, electrical, etc. Not only do you want to see the condition of the property, but you also want to ensure proper maintenance for a safe environment for your tenant. (It is also a great way to make sure the tenant did not sneak in a pet or is smoking in your "no pets & no smoking" property.) When I say periodic, you still must be within reason with your inspection because it's easy to get your tenant thinking that you're making excuses to check upon them. I would say, keep your inspections to no more than 1 per quarter to semi-annually. The phrase "reasonable intervals" is used in a typical rental agreement.

•For you as a Landlord, you may want to create and compile a list of purveyors who you know are reliable and competent. This will enable you to send in a maintenance person in a timely manner. This will also save you LOTS of time and energy flipping through the Yellow Pages or webpage's to find a specialist who can accommodate your needs.

It's best to have a handyman or two, a plumber, a clogged-drain specialist, an electrician, a window guy and a cleaning service on your list.

As a final note on this chapter, I personally run a tight ship by expecting the tenant to pay the rent on time and to take great care of the property. In return, I support their need to have a great place to stay, with a landlord that cares about their safety & comfort.

Chapter Six

Checking Out the Tenant

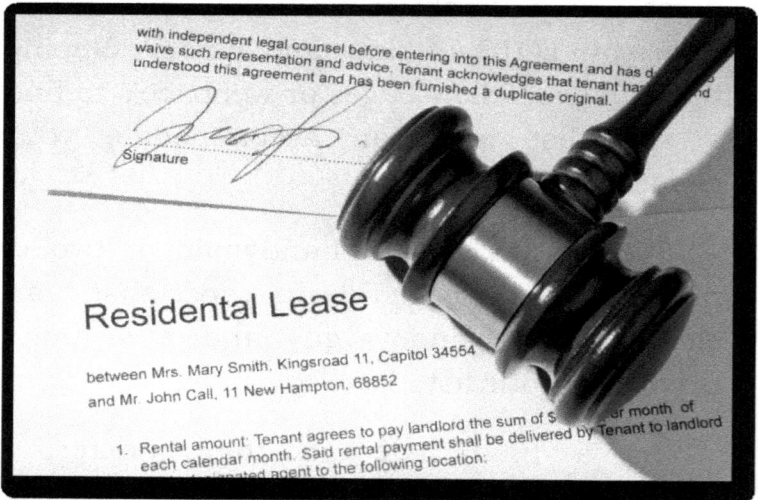

Whether the tenant or you decide to end the relationship, this chapter will apply.

Remember the photos that you made the tenant sign, initial & date? Well, now is the time to bring it back out and inspect the apartment. Also, refer to the "Tenant Check-Out" form to reconcile charges that will be levied against the security deposit. This could include; cleaning, repairs, replacements, utility charges, due rents, etc.

By the way, the Landlord-Tenant Code allows you 14 days to reconcile the charges and return the security deposit to the tenant. Other states may vary, so you might want to review the code in your area.

http://www.landlordtenantcode.gov

Any disputes in charges or property condition discrepancies can end up in small claims court. Bear in mind, that courts tend to favor the "little guy" so have your ducks in line. Make sure that you have the before pictures (at the time of check-in), as well as, the after pictures (at the time of check-out). This kind of evidence is extremely difficult to refute, likely, making it favorable for you.

Always make sure that you have all the keys, fobs, remotes, etc. returned to you and signed off by you. This is the same Keys/Fobs/Remotes/Docs Form from the beginning. It's always a good idea to change door locks after the checkout.

Before parting ways, get the tenant's forwarding address and don't take "No" for an answer. Absolutely refuse to return the security deposit at the time of check out. Wait until you get all invoices and bills before returning the balance of the security deposit. You could find some well-hidden damages and will then regret returning the security deposit upon demand and without a valid forwarding address.

If you have a situation where you actually have to evict a tenant, you must hire a lawyer that specializes in evictions. The attorney will get a court order to evict, and then a hearing will be set for the tenant, where an eviction date will be set. If the tenant cannot be found or simply does not show up, the process will take place anyway with the Sheriff physically removing the tenant and their belongings, which will be put into storage. At this point, you can change the locks and clean the place up to re-rent. This process will cost at least $1,000, depending on how much time is involved. Go to:

http://www.landlordguidance.com/evicti on- notice-forms/

This website will give you the eviction process for each state. The eviction route is pretty rare, as long as you are diligent in your tenant selection.

In Summary

The experience of being a landlord can be one of success and self-actualization or one of failure and dismay. If you follow the advice of this book, you will experience the former.

Good luck on your journey as a successful landlord!